SLED DOGS

BY PHYLLIS RAYBIN EMERT

EDITED BY DR. HOWARD SCHROEDER
Professor in Reading and Language Arts
Dept. of Elementary Education
Mankato State University

PRODUCED & DESIGNED BY
BAKER STREET PRODUCTIONS

CRESTWOOD HOUSE

LIBRARY OF CONGRESS CATALOGING IN PUBLICATION DATA
Emert, Phyllis Raybin.
  Sled dogs.

  SUMMARY: Discusses the history of sled dogs, the characteristics of various sled dog breeds, how they are trained, and the different types of races in which they participate. Includes a glossary of terms.
  1. Sled dogs--Juvenile literature. 2. Sled dog racing--Juvenile literature. (1. Sled dogs. 2. Sled dog racing) I. Schroeder, Howard. II. Title. III. Series.
SF428.7.E44   1985   636.7'0886   85-14967
ISBN 0-89686-288-7 (lib. bdg.)

International Standard Book Number:	Library of Congress Catalog Card Number:
Library Binding 0-89686-288-7	85-14967

ILLUSTRATION CREDITS

Peter Hornby: Cover, 5, 8, 15, 20, 23, 25, 29, 31
Annie Griffiths/DRK Photo: 7, 34, 41
Jim Brandenburg/DRK Photo: 12-13
Central Park Conservancy: 14
Sue Matthews/DRK Photo: 17, 44-45
Don Stenger: 19, 26, 38
D. Cavagnaro/DRK Photo: 22
Stephen J. Krasemann/DRK Photo: 37
Jan Richards: 43

CRESTWOOD HOUSE
Hwy. 66 South, Box 3427
Mankato, MN 56002-3427

Table of contents

"Special thanks to Melissa Robyn and Matthew Brooks."

1.

Togo and Balto

In a kennel near Nome, Alaska, thirty-three sled dogs rested quietly. One was the best-known lead dog in the area. His name was Togo. Togo was light grey with pale blue eyes. He was small for a Siberian Husky and only weighed forty-eight pounds (21.8 kg). But he had won many important races for his master. The twelve-year-old dog was owned by Leonhard Seppala. Many thought Seppala was the best dog "musher" in all of Alaska. (Musher is a name for the driver of a team of sled dogs.)

In that same kennel, there was another dog. This one was a big, all-black, husky with one white foreleg. His name was Balto. Balto was not fast enough to be on Seppala's racing teams. But he was strong and steady. He did his job well, which was hauling freight. These two dogs were soon to become famous throughout the world.

In January of 1925, Nome was a small town of about fifteen hundred people. It was located on the shores of the Bering Sea. Every year in late fall, the sea ice froze, cutting Nome off from the outside world. Travel from town to town was only possible by dog sled. Messages could be sent by telegraph.

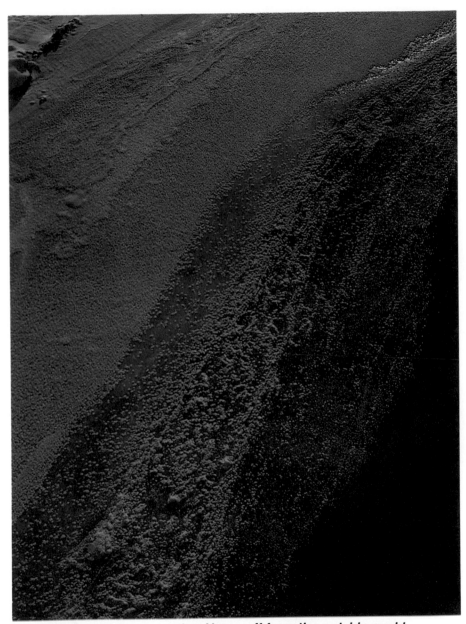

Every fall the sea froze, cutting Nome off from the outside world.

But mail was delivered by dog-team relays. The closest railroad was in Nenana, nearly seven hundred miles (1,129 km) away.

Curtis Welch was the only doctor in Nome. He was upset because two sick Eskimo children had died. "I just don't know why they were ill," Dr. Welch said to his wife. "I can't stop thinking about it." A few days later a six-year-old boy got sick. "Let's have a look," said the doctor. He opened the boy's mouth. Dr. Welch saw patches of white on the boy's throat. "Oh, no," he thought to himself. "It's diphtheria. I don't have enough serum to stop it from spreading." The little boy didn't live through the night. It would only be a matter of time before the deadly disease spread through the town and into the nearby Eskimo villages.

Dr. Welch went to the mayor. "We need more diphtheria serum," he told the city council. "It's the only hope we have to stop an epidemic."

The mayor wired the governor. A hospital in Anchorage was ready to send serum by train to Nenana. The problem was getting it to Nome over hundreds of miles of icy wilderness.

There were only two airplanes in Alaska in 1925. They were biplanes (planes with two wings) with open cockpits. Flying was done only in the summer months. A pilot in an open cockpit might freeze in the winter air.

The governor arranged for dog-team relays to

carry the first shipment of the serum. The best drivers and dogs were chosen to follow the mail delivery route from Nenana to Nome. If the serum didn't arrive in Nome quickly, many people would die.

Leonhard Seppala would drive one of the relay teams. His Siberian Huskies were the fastest dogs in Alaska. Seppala's lead dog was Togo. The leader can follow a trail even if it's covered by snow. They have power over the other dogs on the team. The lead dog obeys the master's commands.

As a puppy, Togo was hard to handle. He was always getting into trouble. When he was eight-months-old, he jumped a high wire fence when he saw Seppala leave with the team. Then he followed the team to a mining camp many miles away. Running loose, Togo bothered the other dogs. So Sep-

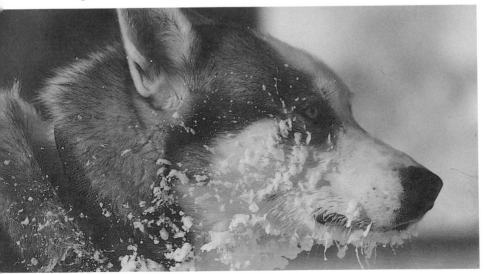

Sled dogs are tough!

7

pala hitched up the frisky pup in the position nearest the sled. The young dog settled down. He worked harder than his full-grown teammates. By the end of the day, Togo was sharing the lead position. He was later to serve Seppala as lead dog for over a dozen years.

The serum arrived at Nenana on the night of January 27. It was packed in a special container. Quilting and then canvas was wrapped around it for protection from the cold. The whole package weighed twenty pounds (9.1 kg).

In Nome, three more people had died. There were fifty more cases of diphtheria. Several teams, includ-

The serum was carefully packed.

ing Seppala's, started south from Nome to meet the serum. Other relay teams traveled north from Nenana, carrying the important package.

"Wild Bill" Shannon started north first. Shannon traveled fifty-two miles (83.9 km) in weather that dropped to nearly -50°F! In extreme cold, mushers must breathe through their noses. A deep breath through the mouth could freeze their lungs. The team must go slowly to prevent frosting of the dog's lungs.

Shannon warmed up the serum in a mail cabin on the trail. Then he gave it to Dan Green for the next leg of the relay. The serum went from Dan Green to Johnny Folger to Sam Joseph. Driver after driver took their turn carrying the precious medicine. The riders rode day and night, trying to get to Nome as soon as possible.

During Charlie Evan's drive, the temperature dropped to -65°F. Two of his dogs began to freeze as they ran. He loaded them on his sled. Then he ran in front trying to help the other seven dogs. The two dogs later died. As the trail headed over the mountains, the weather got worse. But the blinding snow storm didn't stop Evans.

Within minutes of starting his relay leg, Harry Ivanoff met up with Leonhard Seppala. Seppala had driven his team more than 150 miles (242 km) in four days. He took the serum and headed back to Nome.

Seppala soon had to make a difficult decision.

"Should I go straight over the the ice across Norton Bay?" he thought to himself. "These high winds could break up the ice. Then we'd be trapped. But if I go along the coast, I'd lose hours — maybe even a full day." The forty-eight-year-old sled dog racer made up his mind. "We'll take our chances across the Bay," he said to himself.

As they raced forward, the dogs slipped and fell a few times on the slick ice. The sled was even blown over once. In some places the ice was jagged and rough. But it didn't break up. At last they reached the other shore. Seppala stopped to rest that night and warm the serum. The dogs had gone eighty-four miles (135.5 km) that day.

The next morning Seppala looked out at the trail he had taken the day before. It was gone! All he saw were pieces of ice and open water. The wind and snow blinded Seppala, so he let Togo lead the team forward, mile after mile. Togo was able to pick up the scent of the trail.

The epidemic continued to spread in Nome. The Board of Health decided to send two more drivers out to help bring the serum back. Gunnar Kaasen would go to Bluff, and Ed Rohn would go to Point Safety. Rohn would drive the serum the last twenty-one miles back into Nome.

Six-year-old Balto sat quietly back in his kennel. He and twelve other dogs had not been chosen to be part of Leonhard Seppala's relay team. Gunnar

Kaasen, like Seppala, also raced dog sled teams. Kaasen felt that strength in a dog was more important than speed. Balto was strong and reliable. When it came time to choose the lead dog for his team, Kaasen selected the black husky.

When Seppala's dogs finished their leg of the relay, they dropped from exhaustion. Charlie Olson took the serum and headed out. The winds were up to fifty miles an hour. Olson's dogs were nearly frozen when they reached Gunnar Kaasen twenty-five miles away. Olson's fingers were white with frost bite when he gave the serum to Kaasen.

The storm didn't let up as Kaasen's team started out. The wind blew huge drifts. The dogs sank in the deep snow. But Balto was able to pick up the trail. As they crossed the Topkok River, Balto stopped. Kaasen went to see what was wrong. He saw that the big dog was standing in water because the ice had cracked under the snow. Because Balto had stopped so quickly, the other dogs' feet were dry.

Kaasen quickly took Balto into a snowdrift. The snow, rubbed against the pads of his feet, helped to dry them. "Go, Balto," shouted Kaasen as they set off again. Several times gusts of wind flipped over the dogs and sled. Once the serum flew off into a snowbank. For a few seconds, Kaasen was frantic. But he found the package and retied it to the sled.

When Kaasen finally reached Point Safety, Ed Rohn was asleep. He thought Kaasen had stopped to wait out the storm. Instead of waiting for Rohn to dress and hitch his dogs, Kaasen went on to Nome. "I had no idea where we were and couldn't guess," he said in Literary Digest (1925). "I couldn't even see the wheel dog (the one closest to the sled) . . . (Balto) scented the trail through the snow and kept going. Balto . . . brought us through."

At 5:30 in the morning on February 2, the tired, nearly frozen dog sled team entered Nome. Kaasen went right to the hospital. He handed Dr. Welch the serum. It had taken 127½ hours to travel 674 miles

The sled dog teams traveled day and night.

(1,087 km) from Nenana to Nome. The diphtheria epidemic was stopped. There were no more deaths. A week later, a second batch of serum arrived in Nenana. Again, the serum was brought to Nome by dog-team relays.

Newspapers covered the story of the serum race throughout the world. Kaasen's decision to by-pass Ed Rohn and take the serum into Nome is still argued about today. Some feel he wanted glory and publicity. Others believe Kaasen made the right decision.

Balto became a hero. A bronze statue of the big black husky now stands in Central Park in New York City. Balto became the symbol for all the courageous sled dogs and mushers who took part in the serum relay.

The statue of Balto in New York City's Central Park.

14

Togo and Balto were husky's, like this dog.

Seppala and others in Alaska felt that Togo was the real hero of the race. Seppala and Togo went the longest distance. They covered several hundred miles under very hard conditions.

The Dog Musher's Hall of Fame was started in 1966. Among the first to be chosen for this honor were Leonhard Seppala and Togo.

2.

Eskimos were the first mushers

It's not known exactly when dogs were first hitched up to sleds. Many believe the wandering tribes of Siberia were the first to use sled dogs about four thousand years ago. Siberia is a land of extreme cold. Most of the year, snow and ice cover the ground. The people who live in this, and other, northern Arctic areas are called Eskimos.

The Eskimos needed a way to travel from one place to another. They carried food and supplies on sleds, but the snow and cold made it hard to go very far. They started using dogs to help pull their sleds for them.

Many of the Eskimo dogs were bred with wolves. Over the years, they adapted to the cold. The dogs had heavy coats. They were strong and had large padded feet. They could sleep outside in the snow and not freeze. Sled dogs were used by the Eskimos to follow herds of animals, which they hunted for food. Sometimes, they had to go very long distances. Often, more than one dog was hitched up to the sled. More dogs pull heavier loads faster and farther.

More dogs were added to the sled as distances and loads became greater.

17

Some special sled dogs

The North Pole was reached in 1909, by Sir Robert Peary. He wrote that without sled dogs, "It would be folly to think of attempting the conquest of the Great Ice." Roald Amundsen of Norway reached the South Pole in 1911. He stated, ". . . the Eskimo Husky (a sled dog) . . . can overcome terrain (ground) which a tractor can't penetrate and a plane can't land on."

Gold was discovered in Alaska in the late 1800's. In the winter, travel to the gold fields was possible only by dog sled. Sled dogs were used to haul freight and equipment to the mining camps. Mail was delivered by dog sled. (It was 1963, before the U.S. Post Office retired the last dog team in Alaska.)

From 1873 until 1969, the Royal Canadian Mounted Police used dog teams to enforce the law. Teams of sled dogs once pulled supplies and mail in the western mountains of the United States. Some delivered mail. Others rescued lost travelers.

Sled dogs were even used in World War I. Teams of dogs pulled sleds of bullets, shells, and supplies during winter months. Other dog teams transported wounded men to field hospitals. In World War II, the U.S. Army used sled dog teams to rescue airmen shot down in snowy areas. They also hauled supplies. During the Battle of the Bulge, 209 sled dogs were used in rescue work.

Even today, sled dogs can reach places where men and machines still can't go. Scientists on Arctic expeditions depend on sled dogs for travel. In some northern areas, dogs are still used for hunting and transportation.

Sled dog racing

Sled dogs are used for sport, as well as work. The first organized sled dog race was held in 1908, in Alaska. The 408 mile (658 km) race was called the All-Alaska Sweepstakes. As racing became more popular, sleds, harnesses, and lines were built of lighter materials. This allowed the dogs to pull faster. Sled dogs began to be bred for speed, too.

The International Sled Dog Racing Association was formed in 1966. It promotes sled dog racing all over the world. Races are held in the United States, Canada, and Europe. Mushers of all ages race for money, trophies, and just for fun.

Sled dog racing has turned into a sport for everyone.

3.

Special qualities

Sled dogs would rather run in the cold than sleep in a warm kennel. They're born with the strong urge to pull. They adapt easily to being part of a team.

Good sled dogs are strong and fast. They are able to stand extremely cold weather. Sled dogs are hard-working. They must be even-tempered and not fight with the other dogs. The pads of a sled dog's feet must be tough and thick.

The pads of a dog's feet must be tough and thick.

There are many kinds of sled dogs. The most popular pure breeds are the Siberian husky, the Alaskan Malamute, and the Samoyed. Mixed-breeds, such as the Alaskan husky and the village, or Eskimo dog, are also used to pull sleds.

Siberian husky

The Chukchi tribe in Siberia bred a special kind of sled dog. They wanted a dog which could travel fast over long distances, pulling a light load. The Chukchi also valued these dogs as pets. They were kept inside their homes as guards and companions. The Chukchis treated them with care and love. The dogs were gentle and hard-working. They were also strong and fast.

Today, these dogs are called Siberian huskies. They are smaller than the other northern sled dogs.

Siberian huskies are friendly and alert. They're clean, free of dog odor, and make good pets. They have a double coat of thick fur which lies smooth and protects them from the cold. Colors range from pure white to mixes of tan, gray, silver, or black. The head is fox-like, with markings around the face and eyes. The eyes are either brown or blue, or sometimes one of each color. The medium-sized body is very muscular and strong. They run best when pulling average to light loads.

Males are twenty-one to twenty-four inches (54-60.2 cm) high at the shoulders. Females are twenty to twenty-two inches (51.3-56.4 cm) tall. They weigh between thirty-five and sixty pounds (15.9-27.2 kg).

The Siberian husky runs best when pulling average to light loads.

Alaskan Malamute

The Malamute was first discovered by explorers in the tribes of the Mahlamut Eskimos. These Eskimos took good care of their dogs. They bred them for strength and endurance. The dogs can cover long distances and need very little food.

Known as the "workhorse of the North," the Malamute is big and strong. Malamutes are also gentle and good with children. They can be fierce and loyal fighters.

Alaskan Malamutes are known as the "workhorse of the North."

Their feet have thick pads with protective hair between the toes. Their woolly undercoats are thick and oily. The hair can be up to two inches long. The thick, rough outercoat stands out from the body.

Malamutes are light gray to black in color. They have white underbodies. They also have white markings on their legs, feet, and face. Their eyes are always brown. Malamutes have no dog odor and only shed two times a year. They are twenty-three to twenty-five inches tall (59-64 cm) at the shoulder and weigh seventy-five to eighty-five pounds (34.1-38.6 kg).

Samoyed

These dogs are named after the Samoyed tribe which settled in Siberia. Of all breeds, the Samoyed is the most pure. No other dogs or wolves have been cross-bred with them. The Samoyed people used their dogs as hunters, reindeer herders, and sled dogs. They were also used as watchdogs and as pets. Combings from their coats were spun into yarn. The yarn was used to make clothing. At night, the dogs slept inside with the family. This close relationship with man over the years made the Samoyed a gentle and loving family dog.

Sometimes called "Sams," they are very beautiful dogs. Their undercoat is soft, short, and thick.

Sometimes called "Sams," Samoyed dogs are an almost pure breed.

Longer, rough hair grows through it to form the thick outercoat. The hair stands straight out from the body. Their tails are curled and bushy. Thick hair around the neck and shoulders frame the face. The lips curve slightly up at the corners forming a "smile." They're pure white, cream, or light beige in color. Their eyes are dark.

Samoyeds are good working dogs, even in extreme cold. Their large feet have thick, tough pads with protective hair between the toes. Cheerful and

Samoyeds are good working dogs.

26

friendly, they are very smart and loyal. Sams are nineteen to twenty-four inches (48.7-60.2 cm) tall at the shoulder. They weigh between thirty-five and sixty-seven pounds (16-30.5 kg).

Other sled dogs

The word husky is used to describe dogs of mixed northern breeds which pull sleds. Alaskan huskies have been bred from Siberians, Samoyeds, Malamutes, and even wolves. The husky stands twenty-four to twenty-six inches (61.5-66.7 cm) high and weighs between fifty and seventy pounds (22.7-31.8 kg). These dogs are taller than Siberians and weigh less than Malamutes. They are faster and stronger than many other breeds and are often used for sled dog racing.

The Alaskan village dog is also known as the Eskimo dog. They're noted for their speed. The village dog has been bred with whatever dogs (or wolves) were around the village. Some run as fast as seventeen miles an hour. They can be any color. Village dogs are usually tall, about twenty-three to twenty-five inches (59-64 cm) at the shoulder. They only weigh forty-five to fifty pounds (20.5-22.7 kg).

4.

The positions

Each position is important on a sled dog team. The lead dog runs in front. It obeys the musher's commands and guides the team. The two dogs right behind the leader are called point dogs. They help to guide and pace the team. (They're called swing dogs in Alaska.) The pair behind the point dogs are the swing dogs. (They're called team dogs in Alaska.) These dogs have strength and endurance. Closest to the sled are the wheel dogs. Their toughness and power help get the sled going and keep it on the trail.

Harnesses and lines

Every sled dog wears a special harness. The harness fits over the body of the dog so it can run in comfort. The harness lets the dog pull from the shoulders and chest. Different harnesses are used for racing than for freight hauling. A racing harness is light and weighs only a few ounces. Most are made from nylon webbing. A freight hauling harness is heavier and has more parts.

Each sled dog wears a special harness.

The harnessed dog is attached to the sled by lines. Today, the lines are made of polyethylene (plastic) rope. The "gang hitch" is used by most mushers in sled dog racing today. In this hitch, the main towline runs from the sled down the center of the team to the lead dog. The dogs are hitched up to the main towline in pairs. Sometimes single dogs are spaced between the pairs.

A neckline runs from the towline to each dog's collar. The neckline stops the dogs from turning out and bothering other teams. A tugline runs from the main towline to the back of each dog's harness. To connect the lines, toggles, snaps, or loops are used. If there are two leader dogs, they are connected together by a double neckline.

The "fan hitch" connects each of the dogs directly to the sled behind them. The dogs spread out side by side like a fan. The leader has a longer line and keeps out in front. The fan hitch is used to cross Arctic ice and open areas.

Two types of sleds

The sled is a frame built on two runners. The runners help it to travel over the snow without sinking. Racing sleds are made of hard wood like ash, birch, hickory, or maple. They must be light, strong, and flexible. A racing sled weighs about twenty-five to thirty pounds (11.4-13.6 kg). The pieces of the sled are tied together with heavy nylon cord or rawhide. The runners are coated with thick plastic or steel.

Freight sleds are longer and wider than racing sleds. They weigh sixty to one hundred pounds (27.3-45.5 kg). Sometimes they're as long as fourteen feet (4.3 m). They're not built for speed, but to carry heavy loads.

The basket of the sled is used to carry people or supplies. There are handle bars for the musher to grab. The brush bow is a curved piece of wood or plastic. It sticks out in front of the sled. The brush

Racing sleds are light, but strong.

bow protects the sled from anything it might hit. All sleds have a claw brake which can slow and stop the sled. Another way to stop is with a snow hook or brush hook. The snow hook is made from steel. It can be sunk in snow drifts or between ice blocks. The brush hook can hook on to trees and solid objects.

Other equipment

The bottom of the sled basket may be covered with a mat of canvas or carpeting. A dog bag holds an injured dog. It keeps them quiet if the dog must ride on the sled. Only the dog's head sticks out of the bag.

A sled bag carries extra harnesses, lines, gloves, or snow hooks. Coats are carried along for older dogs or those who need protection from the cold. Loin covers protect the dog's undersides if they begin to freeze. Dog boots are made of heavy canvas. They protect the dog's feet and pads from jagged ice.

Some drivers carry short three-foot (1 m) whips. The dogs react to the sound of the snapping whip. Other drivers carry whistles or bottle caps strung together (called jinglers) to get the dog's attention.

5.

Training a puppy

The ways of training sled dogs differ from one musher to another. Some start with a young puppy. When a puppy is three or four weeks old, it's handled and played with each day. Members of the family, friends, and even strangers, touch and speak with the pup. The pup starts to connect people with having fun. It's given a name which is repeated again and again.

At six to eight weeks of age, a harness and collar are put on the pup. A rope is attached to the harness. The pup drags it along while it plays. After awhile, a light block of wood or other object is tied to the rope.

Later, a leash is attached to the pup's collar. The trainer runs alongside, letting the puppy go where it wants. The pup is urged to pull the block along. Training should always be fun for the dog. Five to ten minute sessions, twice a day, are enough for a puppy. After a time, the pup pulls the block without the leash. As the puppy gets older, heavier weights are added. By the time the pup is five months old, it can pull around a car tire.

The trainer says, "No" when the puppy does something wrong. When something is done right,

Future sled dogs!

the trainer says, "Good." The pup should hear happiness in the trainer's tone of voice when being praised. The dog must know it has pleased its master. When the pup runs in the harness, the trainer says, "Hike" or "Go Ahead." When the dog stops, the trainer says, "Whoa." This gets the puppy used to basic sled dog commands at a very young age.

Champion sled dog racer, George Attla, of Alaska, starts training his pups when they are three or four months old. He has the pups run behind the sled. They may run several miles while following the team. It becomes an exciting game for the dogs. They look forward to running.

The first team run

When the pup is six to eight months old, it's hitched up to the team for its first real run. A level trail in good weather is best. For the first run, some mushers put two pups with an experienced lead dog. George Attla hooks up four adult dogs with four puppies.

The young pup is taken out a few times each week with the team. They run short distances of one to two miles. The dog is tried at different positions. One may run best right behind the leader. Another may do well next to the sled or near a certain dog.

Training an adult dog

Two methods are used to train an older dog to pull a sled — pulling first or speed first.

Training a dog to pull first, begins with a line tied to the collar. At first, the trainer runs alongside, then lets the dog run in front, pulling at a steady speed. The trainer says "Go" or "Hike" when the dog starts, and "Whoa" when it stops. Praising after a good run makes the dog look forward to the next training session.

The next step is to add a harness. The trainer runs alongside with a line to the collar. When the dog begins to pull out in front, the trainer switches to a line attached to the back of the harness. Then the trainer drops back behind the dog. This lets the dog get the feel of pulling in the harness.

A light load is then attached to the harness line. The trainer runs alongside and then behind the dog. Heavier loads are used until the trainer can't keep up with the dog. Then a switch is made to a sled or training vehicle.

The trainer who teaches speed first (before pulling) uses a sled or vehicle at the beginning of training. If there is snow, the dog is hitched to a sled. If there is no snow, a three-wheeled, training cart can be used.

The new dog is hooked up with a trained team in the wheel position. The first runs are slow and short.

As the other dogs get used to the new adult dog, he is moved to different positions and the runs get longer.

Getting in shape

After the dogs have been put together as a team, they learn to run longer distances. They start slowly, building up their strength and toughening their feet. Some drivers train the dogs to run the same distance that a race will be. Others train the dogs for far longer distances than they will race. George Attla changes the distance each day, so the dogs don't know what to expect. At the beginning, the dogs go

The dogs run longer distances each day.

on short runs each day. As they cover longer distances, they only run three to five times a week.

Weather which is too warm can be dangerous for the dogs. Many mushers begin training in October when the weather is cool. In many parts of Alaska there's snow on the ground by this time. By early January, the dogs are fully trained and ready for the racing season.

Commands

Drivers control their dog teams by voice or other sound commands. They have no reins to hold. To

Drivers do not use reins to control the dogs.

start the team, the musher says "Hike" or "Let's Go" in an excited way. "Gee" means right turn. "Haw" means left turn. "Gee Over" means a little to the right. "Haw Over" means a little to the left. "Easy" means to slow down. "Whoa" means stop. "Straight Ahead" and "Stay" mean just what they say. To speed up, the driver says "Get up."

Along with the command, a whistle, whip, or jingler is used to get the dog's attention. If the musher wants a certain dog to speed up, the dog's name will be used first. Turn commands are given to the leader, whose name is used. The turn command is repeated a few times before the turn is actually reached. If commands are followed correctly, the trainer says "Good" and the dog's name. Drivers only talk to their dogs when giving commands. Otherwise, it's quiet on the trail.

Training lead dogs

The lead dogs follow the commands of the driver. They're very smart, strong, and fast. Lead dogs enjoy running in the front of the team. They keep the lines tight between the dogs. The rest of the team respect and follow the leaders. Lead dogs can be male or female.

Most drivers begin lead dog training at three to four months. The pup is run in harness down a trail.

The trainer runs behind. As the dog gets close to a crossing, the trainer steps off to the right. The trainer pulls the line and says "Gee." When the pup moves in the right direction, the dog is praised. "Gee" turns are repeated again and again until the pup understands the command. Then "Haw" turns are taught. If the pup makes a mistake, the trainer stops and says, "No." The leash is pulled in the correct direction and the command is given again. The pup is praised when it's done correctly. Other commands are taught using the same method.

As the leader learns the commands, more dogs are added behind it. Sometimes, two leaders-in-training are hitched into a double lead. George Attla, and others, train new leaders along with an older, experienced leader. The new dog follows the old one and learns quickly. After a time, the new lead dog goes out on the trail with a whole team.

The lead dog learns to pass other sleds head-on. They also overtake and pass sleds in front of them. Training a lead dog to pass takes much practice.

Drivers

Good balance is needed to ride a dog sled. When riding, drivers bend their knees and lean forward. They move with the sled. Mushers run alongside or behind the sled over rough ground or sharp curves.

This stops the sled from tipping over and helps the dogs.

Mushers slow the sled down by dragging a foot. The sled is steered by shifting the driver's weight onto one runner or twisting the frame of the sled (called warping). Drivers also lean to the inside on curves.

Sometimes the driver will "pedal" to help the dogs. One foot is kept on the runner while the other foot pushes the ground. Each push must be timed exactly or the sled will jerk and slow the dogs.

This Alaskan musher stops to rest his dogs near Mt. McKinley.

6.

Racing

The longest race is the Iditarod Trail Race. This race began in Alaska in 1973. The trail goes from Anchorage to Nome and is 1,049 miles (1,692 km) long. The race takes from two to four weeks. Part of it goes over the old mail delivery trail which connected the gold mining camps in the early 1900's.

Most races are not over fifty miles (80.6 km) long. They're usually run over two to three days. A number of important races are held in Alaska. A few take place in Canada. Other big races are held in New Hampshire, Idaho, Minnesota, New York, and Michigan.

A family sport

In addition to men, women and children also take part in sled dog racing. In March, 1985, twenty-eight-year-old Libby Riddles became the first woman to win the Iditarod Trail Race. Riddles took over the lead in a blinding blizzard.

Young children take part in the junior musher races. A child can move from the one-dog class up to

Dog sledding can be a family sport. This family is using a three-wheeled training cart.

the two, three, and five-dog events over time. In Alaska, one-dog mushers can be as young as three years old. But most junior events start at age six. Junior races are a quarter mile for one-dog teams and up to one mile (1.6 km) for three-dog teams.

The starting line of the Iditarod Trail Race.

Weight and freight pulls

In weight pulling contests, sled dogs compete against other dogs in their own weight class. These are dogs that are too large for racing. Many are Alaskan Malamutes. They have one to two minutes to pull a load a certain distance (from twenty to fifty feet) (6.1 M to 15.2 M). The dogs wear a heavy harness. Their owners stand in front or at the dog's shoulder. They talk to the dogs, urging them to pull.

These larger dogs also take part in freight racing. Forty or fifty pounds (18.2 to 22.7 kg) of weight for each dog in the team is loaded onto a large sled. Freight races are up to a few miles long. Teams of one, two, or three dogs compete against other teams of the same size. These events are very popular.

In conclusion

For thousands of years sled dogs have helped people. Today, they're used more for sport and recreation. But in cold and snowy regions, modern machines can break down. It's good to know that the sled dog can still get through.

Glossary

BASKET — *The part of the sled which holds people and supplies.*

BRUSH BOW — *Curved piece of wood or plastic which acts as a bumper in the front of the sled.*

DIPHTHERIA — *A severe disease with weakness, high fever, and breathing trouble.*

EPIDEMIC — *A disease that spreads fast.*

GANG HITCH — *Dogs hitched to the main towline in pairs; used by most mushers in sled dog racing today.*

JINGLER — *About ten or twelve bottle caps strung together on a wire; gets the dog's attention when shaken.*

LEAD DOG — *The dog in the front of the team; guides the other dogs and obeys the commands of the driver.*

MUSHER — *Another name for the driver of a dog team; from the French word, marcher, meaning to walk or march.*

NECKLINE — *Line which connects each dog's collar to the main towline.*

POINT DOGS — *The two dogs hitched right behind the lead dog; also called swing dogs in Alaska.*

RUNNER — *Long, thin piece of wood, on which a sled slides over the snow.*

SERUM — *A fluid injected into a person to prevent disease;*

SWING DOGS — *The two dogs hitched behind the point dogs; also called team dogs in Alaska.*

TOWLINE — *The main line which runs from the sled down the center of the dog team, also called a gangline.*

TUGLINE — *The line which connects the back of each dog's harness to the main towline.*

WHEEL DOGS — *The two dogs hitched nearest to the sled.*

WORKING DOGS

*READ ABOUT THE MANY KINDS
OF DOGS THAT WORK FOR A LIVING:*

**HEARING-EAR
DOGS**

**GUIDE
DOGS**

**WATCH/GUARD
DOGS**

**LAW
ENFORCEMENT
DOGS**

**SEARCH
& RESCUE
DOGS**

**STUNT
DOGS**

**SLED
DOGS**

**MILITARY
DOGS**

CRESTWOOD HOUSE